The Little Book of Parachute Play

Making and using parachutes in the Foundation Stage

by Clare Beswick
Illustrations by Martha Hardy

LITTLE BOOKS WITH BIG IDEAS

Published 2011 by A&C Black Publishers Limited
36 Soho Square, London W1D 3QY
www.acblack.com

ISBN 978-1-9041-8780-6

A CIP record for this publication is available from the British Library.

Printed in Great Britain by Latimer Trend & Company Limited

This book is produced using paper that is made from wood grown in managed, sustainable forests. It is natural, renewable and recyclable.

The logging and manufacturing processes conform to the environmental regulations of the country of origin.

Contents

Introduction

A parachute can be a wonderful resource used everyday in your setting, or sadly it may linger collecting dust at the back of a cupboard – taking up valuable storage space. With a little planning and preparation a parachute can be used regularly to support everyone's learning from the youngest children just setting out on the foundation stage to those who are busily pushing the boundaries of Key Stage 1, ready for more.

First impressions may leave you thinking a parachute is a piece of equipment most suited to promoting physical development, or perhaps goals within the personal, social and emotional development area of learning. In fact, it can be effectively used to promote learning in all six areas. It is versatile and can be used for lively active play, to support imaginative play and creativity, to promote listening and attention skills, to build children's understanding of mathematical ideas and concepts, to support them in communication and literacy skills and much more.

This book provides a wealth of activities and play ideas across all six areas of learning. All the activities are easy to do, with clear concise instructions, using resources readily to hand in most settings.

This book is intended for everyone working in the foundation stage, in schools, preschool playgroups, nurseries and at home.

All the activities:

- are carefully planned to help children make progress towards the Early Learning Goals
- cover all six areas of learning
- are practical and easy to do
- can be easily adapted for children at different developmental stages.

On each activity page there are step-by-step instructions for one main activity, with the key words that you and the children will be using. The early learning goals are clearly shown. The main activity is supplemented by more ideas – at least four further parachute play activities. These will give you plenty of inspiration to support younger children and extend the learning of others.

No parachute? Not a problem!

If you don't already have a parachute, with a little time it is entirely possible to create your own parachute from inexpensive materials. Before embarking on making your own, why not contact your local toy library or Sure Start programme to check out the possibility of borrowing a parachute.

Look at the end of the book for websites, suppliers and Toy Library addresses.

For many of the games you can improvise with just a large flat sheet, but to make the most of the activities and ideas, why not have a go at making a parachute of your own?

To make your own parachute

You will need

- a sewing machine
- a large sheet or roll of tracing paper or greaseproof paper, about 150cm square, for the template
- light fabric, 1 metre wide, in several colours if possible
- scissors
- a metre rule and a protractor for measuring 60 degree angles.

Choosing the fabric

Look for two or three different plain colours of the fabric. Check out the strength of the weave and also the ease with which it can be machine stitched. Choose the same weight of fabric in each colour.

What to do

(The first instruction is the hardest bit!)

1. Draw a triangle template on the tracing paper, with the two long sides 110cm long. You may need to tape two pieces of paper together to make it big enough. Use the protractor to check that the angle at the top corner of the triangle is 60 degrees.

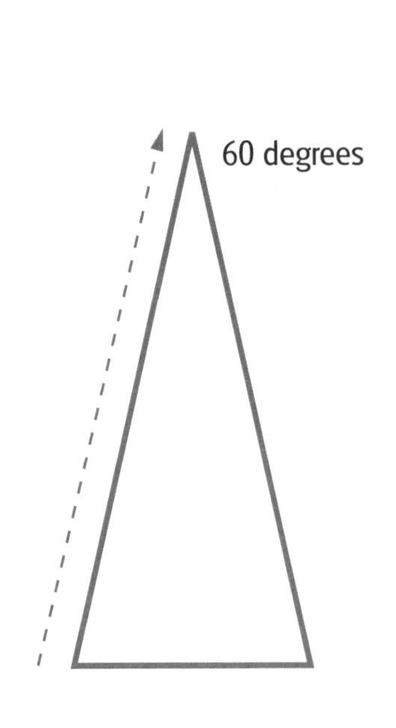

2. Pin your template to the fabric and cut out six triangles, two or three of each colour.
3. Turn the pieces over and iron a seam or hem of 10cm on each side of each triangle. This makes it easier to sew.
4. Check the measurements once more. When the edges are turned over, each side of the triangles needs to be one metre (100cm) long.
5. Now simply machine stitch the triangles together to form a flat circle of fabric. Complete the parachute by machine stitching the outer hem to prevent fraying.

This will make a parachute 2 metres in diameter.

Why not?

- Attach fabric letters, numbers or shapes with Velcro to each triangle.
- Add small bells to the outside edge.
- Trim with different textured ribbons.
- Line with black fabric and Velcro on fabric stars.
- Add some loops to make it easier for children to hang on.
- Make a really huge chute, say 5m in diameter, for parachute play in large areas when you have several adults available to help.

Play safe – safety tips for parachute play

- Choose the area for play carefully. The surface should be clean and smooth, as many parachute activities involve crawling, kneeling and sitting on the floor.
- Make sure that there is plenty of space free of obstacles around the parachute.
- Make sure the children are dressed appropriately for active play.
- Keep the room cool, or play outside on a cool day. Children can get very hot during parachute play.
- Plan the session so that it flows smoothly, with all children remaining on task, clear about the activities and what is expected.
- Start each session with a reminder of how to play safe.

Rules may include:

"Listen carefully"

"Look after your neighbour"

"Stop straight away when asked"

Keep your instructions short, clear and easy to follow.

- Plan a calm activity to end the session. Why not try:
  - sitting on the edge of the chute and passing a handshake around the circle
  - lying very still under the parachute while the adults waft the parachute gently up and down
  - sitting around the edge of the chute, eyes closed, listening for their names to be called so they may go.
  - walking around with the parachute at waist height, gradually moving more and more slowly until you all stop and gently rest the parachute on the floor
  - lying on the parachute listening to some gentle relaxing music.

Remember

Young children left to play unsupervised could become tangled in the parachute. There is a risk of suffocation, or at a best a serious fright. Do not allow children to play without direct adult supervision.

Ten in the bed

Try this great activity just for fun – but it is also really good for counting and talking about one less.

What you need:

- a parachute
- ten children
- a tambourine or shaker

Early Learning Goals:

- say and use number names in order in familiar contexts. (PSRN)
- count reliably up to ten everyday objects. (PSRN)
- find one more and one less than a number from one to ten. (PSRN)
- use mathematical language in play. (PSRN)

What you do:

1. Spread the parachute out flat on the floor, and with the children's help carefully fold the parachute in half to make a semi-circle shape. Talk about the different shapes and colours you can see. What other semi-circles can you find?
2. Ask the children to slide under the straight edge of the parachute, lying flat on their backs next to each other, with just their heads sticking out, as if they were ten children in a bed.
3. Sing the 'Ten in the Bed' song. When you sing 'roll over, roll over', help the first child to roll over, and out from under the parachute. Help them to count how many children are left.
4. Give this child the tambourine or shaker and sing the next verse – 'There were nine in the bed....' When you get to 'roll over', shake the tambourine and help the next child to roll out. Take turns, counting the remaining children and shaking the tambourine.
5. Before the next verse, ask the children how many will be left when another child rolls out. Talk about one less, or perhaps even two less.

And another idea...

- Play this game with lots of teddies. Guess how many teddies are in bed? Estimate and then count to check.
- Play this game with lots of children and change the verses to 'there were children in the bed, and the little one said sit up/roll onto your tummies/curl up small/stretch your arms in the air/show me ten fingers ...' and so on.
- Guess and count how many teddies or children you need head to toe to go right across the parachute. How many are needed if you fold the parachute in half or quarters?
- Hide several balls under the parachute. Lay the parachute down and ask the children to guess. Then count how many balls they can see hiding under the parachute? Take one away and see how many are left.

Vocabulary

- circle
- straight
- curve
- half
- less
- more
- semi-circle

Rainbow fun

Use your parachute and some balloons to play this game for exploring colour and pattern.

What you need:

- a parachute
- lots of balloons (all colours)
- balloon pump
- some coloured stickers

Early Learning Goals:

- look closely at similarities and differences, patterns and change. (KUW)
- notice and comment on patterns. (KUW)
- observe and use positional language. (PSRN)

What you do:

1. Blow up some balloons with the pump.
2. Spread the parachute out on the floor and ask the children to sit down around the edge and gently hold the edge of the parachute. Pull it tight and lift it just a few centimetres off the floor.
3. Ask the children to call out the colour of the balloons as they are thrown on to the parachute. Throw red, then blue, then red again, then blue again and so on. Stop sometimes and ask the children which colour should come next.
4. Play again, extending the activity by using a sequence of three different colours of balloons.
5. Get some blue and some red stickers. Put either a blue or a red sticker on one hand of each child.
6. Ask each child to find a balloon the same colour and then to sit around the edge of the parachute to make a red–blue–red– blue pattern.
7. Help the children to take turns around the circle to call out their colour and throw their balloon onto the parachute.

Tips: Buy tiny coloured stickers from office stationers. Don't over inflate the balloons – it makes them harder to grasp and catch.

And another idea...

- Lay the parachute flat and match a balloon to each coloured section of the parachute.
- Throw lots of different balloons under the parachute. Using a colour dice or spinner, take turns to throw or spin, and crawl under the parachute to find a matching balloon.
- Put different colour stickers on the balloons, such as a red balloon with a green sticker. Roll the balloons onto the top of the parachute. Shake the parachute gently so that one falls off. Ask a child to retrieve it and name the colours.

Collect any burst balloons immediately. They are a potential choking hazard for small children.

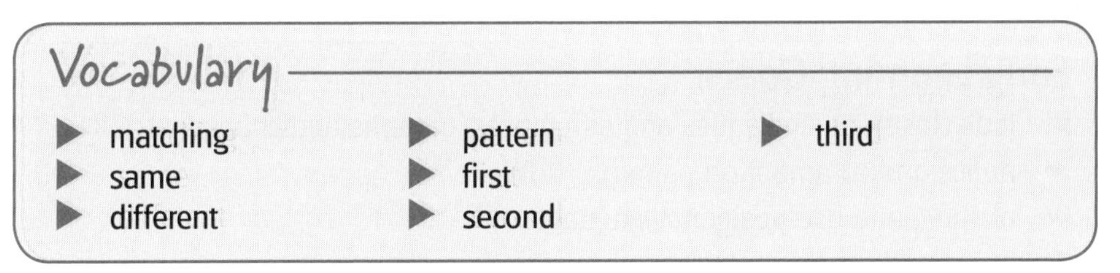

Skip this way, skip that way

Use this game to improve skipping techniques and to practise taking turns and working together.

What you need:

- a name card for each child
- a parachute

Early Learning Goals:

- display high levels of involvement in activities. (PSED)
- form good relations with adults and peers. (PSED)
- relate to and make attachments to members of their group. (PSED)
- ascribe meaning to marks; begin to recognise names and other words. (CLL)
- enjoy dancing and ring games. (CD)

What you do:

1. Shuffle the name cards and put them face down in a pile on the floor.
2. Spread the parachute out on the floor and ask the children to sit around the edge of the parachute, grip the edge and slowly stand up.
3. Wave the parachute up and down together.
4. Choose a child to skip around the edge of the parachute, to the pile of name cards. Ask them to take the top card.
5. Help them to read the name card. Perhaps they can recognise the first letter. The child then skips under the parachute to the child whose name is on the card.
6. The two children then skip around under the parachute as the other children hold the parachute high in the air and sing. You can use 'Here we go Looby Lou, here we go Looby Light, here we go Looby Lou, all on a Saturday night' – or another song.
7. Encourage the children who are skipping to hold hands and skip together. When the song finishes, the child closest to them is the next child to choose a name card and partner.

And another idea...

- Hold on to the parachute together at about waist height as you all walk around in a circle, then put left legs, right legs, etc. in the circle (to 'The Hokey Cokey' if you like).
- Play some music, wafting the parachute up and down. When the music stops turn over two name cards. Call out (or help the children to call out) the names. The two named children then run and swap places under or around the edge of the parachute before the music starts again.
- Place all the name cards face up on the floor. Hold the parachute about 50cm above the floor, and let the children take turns to dive under the parachute to find their name.

Vocabulary

- skip
- fast
- slow
- left
- high
- low

Criss cross

A game for rolling, creeping, crawling and exchanging places under a folded parachute.

What you need:

- a parachute
- 3 sound makers - e.g. a bell, shaker, wooden blocks, drum
- 3 adults

Early Learning Goals:

- move in a variety of ways, move with control and co-ordination. (PD)
- adjust speed and change direction to avoid obstacles. (PD)
- experiment with different ways of moving. (PD)
- sustain attentive listening, responding with comments, questions, and actions. (CLL)

What you do:

1. Play the different sound makers and let the children practise listening to them. Talk about the different sounds.
2. Choose a movement for each sound – e.g. roll over when you hear the bells, crawl to the drum, commando crawl on tummies to the wood block, etc. When the sound stops, the children must stop moving.
3. Try this out, helping any children who need it.
4. Now lay the parachute flat on the floor. With the children's help, fold it in half and then roll it into a long sausage shape.
5. Help each child to find a partner, or form them into groups of three. Hold the rolled up parachute about 50cm above the floor. You need an adult to hold each end.
6. Now one adult plays an instrument to signal the actions for the first pair or group of children. The children roll, creep or crawl under the chute as the instrument plays.
7. Take turns for each group to travel under the rolled up parachute.

And another idea...

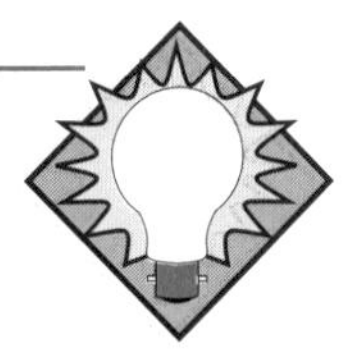

- Change the sound and action several times as the children are travelling under the chute, so they change from crawling to creeping, and so on.
- Play this game with lots of children and change the verses to 'There were children in the bed, and the little one said sit up/roll onto your tummies/curl up small/stretch your arms in the air/show me ten fingers...' and so on.
- Try the game with bunny hops, slithering, and crawling using hands and feet, but no knees on the floor!
- Play the game with the children travelling backwards.
- Try calling out different animal names, so perhaps the first child slithers along under the rolled up parachute as a snake, then the next flies through like a bird, or swims along like a fish, and so on.

Vocabulary

- space
- stretch
- reach
- under
- creep
- crawl
- travel

Matching pairs

Use your parachute to explore different ways of matching and sorting pictures and objects.

What you need:

- a parachute
- 2 each of a selection of objects (socks, keys, hats, etc.)
- matching pairs

Early Learning Goals:

- ask simple questions; use talk to gain attention and exchange ideas. (CLL)
- use and extend vocabulary, exploring the meanings of new words. (CLL)
- describe objects and purposes. (CLL)
- sort objects by function. (KUW)

What you do:

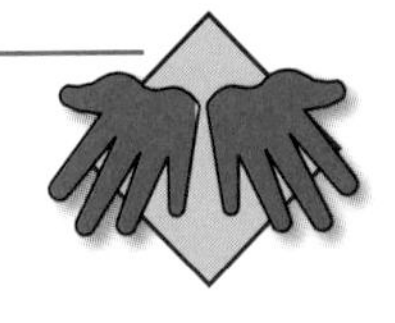

1. Place the pairs of objects on the floor and lay out the parachute over the top. Sit around the edge of the parachute with the children.
2. Let the children take turns diving under the parachute to find an object. When everyone has had a turn, talk about the different objects and match the pairs.
3. Put all the objects back under the parachute.
4. Now ask one child to dive under the parachute and find a particular object. Name it, or describe the object by its use, such as 'Can you find me something to open doors?'.
5. Ask the next child to dive under and find the matching object – e.g. the other key. Make it more exciting by counting to ten (slowly) with the other children to see if the diver can find the object before you all reach ten!
6. Try playing the game with picture and object pairs – e.g. a picture of a key and a real key.
7. Place the picture cards face up on the floor. Ask each child in turn to take a card and find the matching object under the parachute.

And another idea...

- Ask all the children to remove one shoe and place them under the parachute. Hold the parachute at waist height with the children and walk around in a circle. Call the names of three or four children, who then dive under the parachute to find and put on their lost shoe! Make sure all the shoes are clearly marked with their owner's name!
- Place circle, square, triangle and rectangle shaped blocks on the floor. Lay the parachute carefully over the top. Ask each child to find a shape and, feeling through the fabric, count how many sides and corners it has. What is the shape called? What else can you see that is the same shape?
- Put pairs of socks, gloves and dressing up box shoes under the parachute. Take turns to dive under to choose one item and put it on, till all the children are wearing pairs of clothing.

Vocabulary

- pair
- single
- many
- different
- same
- other
- like

Colour swap

A parachute game for finding, using and recognising colours.

What you need:

- small bricks (2 of each colour) enough for 1 per child
- a parachute

Early Learning Goals:

- sustain attentive listening, responding to what they have heard by relevant actions. (CLL)
- be confident to try new activities, initiate ideas and speak in a group. (PSED)
- work as part of a group. (PSED)
- negotiate space successfully when playing games with others. (PD)

What you do:

1. Lay out the parachute flat on the floor.
2. Stand around the edge of the parachute.
3. Ask each child in turn to call out the colour of the segment of the parachute they are standing next to.
4. Call out one of the parachute colours and the name of a child standing next to a segment of that colour. This child then runs round the edge of the parachute to the next segment of the same colour.
5. He or she gently (!) touches the child already standing by this segment on the shoulder and takes their place. This child then needs moves to the next segment of the same colour, touches that child, takes their place and so on.
6. Play this game for each colour on the parachute, so that all the children have a turn.
7. Count out enough coloured bricks for each child to have one. Use an even number of each colour. Give out the bricks. Ask the children to call out in turn the colours of their bricks.
8. Next, you call out one of the colours and the two (or four) children holding that colour race under the parachute to swap places. Keep calling colours and swapping places. Keep the pace brisk.
9. Encourage the children to remember the colour of the brick in their hand – can they play without looking?

And another idea...

- Vary the game by changing the colours and where the children are standing.
- Hold the parachute very close to the floor, so the children swapping places need to slither across under the chute.
- Try the game with cards with different patterns – such as squiggles, zig zags, chequer boards, dots and so on.
- Play the game with different colour shapes, e.g. red circles, or blue squares. The children with the same colour shapes swap.

Vocabulary

- swap
- change
- turn
- listen
- remember
- colours
- shape
- under

Popcorn

Work together to bounce balloons and balls on, off, under and over the parachute in this popular game.

What you need:

- beach balls, balloons or rolled up pairs of socks (or a mixture of these)
- a parachute

Early Learning Goals:

- display high levels of involvement in an activity. (PSED)
- work as part of a group, taking turns and sharing fairly. (PSED)
- use talk to connect, explain and anticipate. (CLL)
- ask questions about why things happen and how things work. (KUW)

What you do:

1. Spread the parachute flat on the floor.
2. Ask the children to stand around the edge and lift the parachute up to waist height.
3. Start by throwing a balloon into the middle. Shake the parachute up and down together, and see how quickly you can get the balloon to bounce off the parachute.
4. Now throw lots of balloons on the parachute and play again.
5. Experiment with big and small movements, wafting the parachute high and low, or make little shakes and shudders. Ask the children to predict what might happen to the balloons with each sort of movement.
6. Try it again with the beach balls. How high will they bounce? What about rolled up pairs of socks? Are they heavier or lighter, larger or smaller?
7. Put them all on together. Which will bounce off first? What will be last to fall?

And another idea...

- Use a marker pen to write each child's name on a balloon. Throw all the balloons onto the parachute. Shake it and see which name comes off first. Which one is last to bounce off the chute?
- Write each child's name on a strip of paper and bounce these like popcorn on the parachute. Each child can throw their name back on the parachute as it is bounced off.
- Use a large beach ball and work together to roll it back and forth across the parachute. Can you make the ball go through the central hole in the parachute (if there is one)?
- Put a soft teddy bear or other soft toy on the parachute. Bounce the toy gently up and down.
- See how high you can bounce the soft toy without letting it fall off the parachute.

Vocabulary

- heavy
- light
- high/low
- big/small
- fast
- slow
- shudder
- waft

In the bucket you go!

Use this game with rules, to give practice in working together to make something happen. This game is more difficult than it looks!

What you need:

- a small blanket (not a parachute)
- a bucket
- teddies and other soft toys
- small balls (sponge/plastic)

Early Learning Goals:

- travel backwards and sideways as well as forwards. (PD)
- move with control and co-ordination. (PD)
- show awareness of space for themselves and others. PD)
- collaborate in devising and sharing tasks, including those with rules. (PD)

What you do:

1. Choose two children to hold the blanket and two more to hold the bucket. They need to stand near the parachute, one pair on each side.
2. Ask the rest of the children to hold the parachute tightly and step backwards so that the parachute is held taut and as flat as possible.
3. Put some balls on the parachute and work together with the children to tip the parachute gently so that the balls roll towards the edge for the other children to catch on the blanket or in the bucket. You probably need to say which!
4. Stop and talk about what happened and how the children needed to move.
5. Try again and see if talking has improved their techniques.
6. Now put some teddies or soft toys on the blanket. Can you tip or roll them on to the blanket or into the bucket?
7. Talk again about which way the parachute needs to be tipped. Try fast and slow movements, high and low.

And another idea...

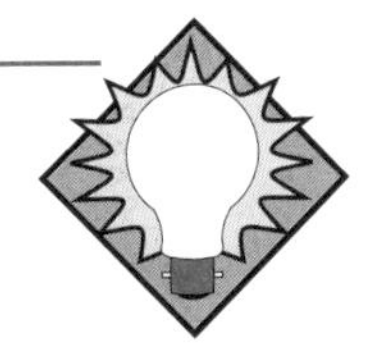

- Put three soft toys on the stretched taut parachute and bounce them up and down as you sing 'Three Little Monkeys Bouncing on the Bed'.
- Put a doll on the parachute and rock the doll while you sing, 'Rock a Bye Baby' or other lullabies.
- Hide some large soft toys under the parachute. Can you guess from the shape and feel of each what it is?
- Hold the parachute and try to move the whole chute forwards, backwards or sideways. Can you all move into the middle so the parachute folds on the floor and then step slowly backwards until it is taut? Try this on tip-toes, with giant strides or tiny steps.
- Work together to practice wafting the parachute really high, so it catches a lot of air. You will need this trick for some of the games later in this book!

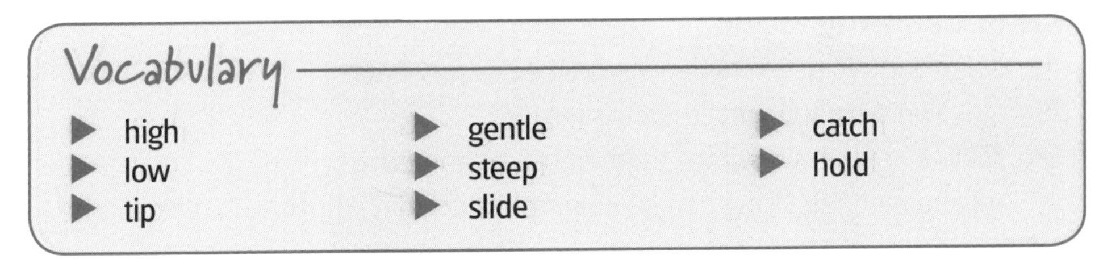

Vocabulary

- high
- low
- tip
- gentle
- steep
- slide
- catch
- hold

Rocket man!

Jet off into space with this number rhyme and game. It helps with counting backwards and 'one more', 'one less'.

What you need:

- just a parachute

Early Learning Goals:

- use some number names accurately in play. (PSRN)
- enjoy joining in with number rhymes and songs; use mathematical language. (PSRN)
- find one more and one less than a number from 1 to 10. (PSRN)
- listen to favourite rhymes and songs, join in with refrains. (CLL)

What you do:

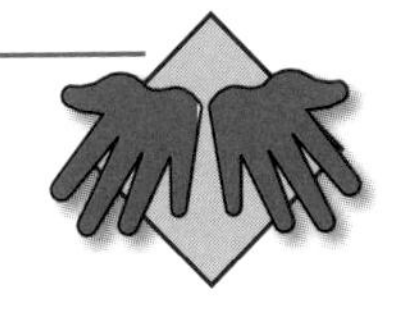

1. Hold the parachute at waist height.
2. Invite five children to be space travellers and to spin around on flying saucers under the parachute.
3. Allow the children to try gently spinning around, but encourage them to sit down and wave their arms too, to avoid anyone becoming dizzy and falling.
4. With the remaining children, walk around in a circle holding the parachute taut to make the sky above.
5. Sing the 'Five Little Spacemen' song (words at end of book).
6. At the end of each verse, invite one of the 'spacemen' to join you holding the parachute.
7. Focus on counting, talking about how many and one less as you count the remaining spacemen.

And another idea...

- Try a rocket launch. Hold the parachute taut and count down with the children from 10 to zero, and blast off. On zero, waft the parachute high in the air, let go and shout blast off. Stand back to avoid the parachute as it falls!
- Make some stars and planets with paper, scissors, paint and collage. Fix these to the inside of the parachute using ribbon or double sided sticky tape. Waft the chute gently up and down as you sing 'Twinkle, Twinkle Little Star'.
- 'Mushroom' the decorated parachute (waft it high in the air, step quickly in and pull it sharply down behind you). The trapped air will create an air filled tent or mushroom, and you will be inside! Sit on the edge of the parachute, in the decorated tent and read Whatever Next by Jill Murphy (Macmillan Children's Books), or Q Pootle 5 by Nick Butterworth (Picture Lions).

Vocabulary

- space
- journey
- dizzy
- spinning
- stars
- planets
- moon
- floating

In my tent

Use your parachute to explore different ways of counting, matching and sorting pictures and objects.

What you need:

- just a parachute

Early Learning Goals:

- experiment with different ways of moving. (PD)
- combine and repeat a range of movements. (PD)
- move with control and co-ordination. (PD)
- have a positive approach to new experiences. (PSED)

What you do:

1. Spread the parachute out on the floor and ask the children to stand around the edge.
2. Lift the parachute as high as you can and, as it fills with air, all take a step forward and pull the parachute down behind you. Quickly sit down with the edge of the parachute tucked firmly under you. The parachute will form an air filled dome or mushroom-like tent.

Encourage the children to stay seated – if they stand up the air will escape and the tent will collapse!

3. Sing an action song to the tune of 'Here We go Round the Mulberry Bush' putting in the actions:
   'This is the way we pat the tent'
   '.... stamp our feet' '.... wave our hands' '.... shake our heads'
4. Take plenty of time to complete and repeat several verses.

Tips: Remember it will get hot under the parachute – so keep the game short, and finish with a second game of gently wafting the parachute up and down and then resting and relaxing to some quiet music at the end. Some children (and adults) may feel uncomfortable in a confined space. Be ready to collapse the tent and start again, or vary the game to meet the needs of everyone.

And another idea...

- Ask the children to wriggle round so that they are facing the edge of the tent. Roll backwards so that their legs are up the side of the tent. Start with a gentle patting of feet on the side of the tent, then get faster and faster, till they are patting as fast and high as they can go.
- Make a tent and pass a ball from child to child as quickly as possible. Add music to the game, passing the ball from child to child and stopping when the music stops.
- Make a tent again and pat balloons back and forth. See how far the children can stretch to retrieve the balloons with out letting the tent collapse.
- Pass an action (e.g. wriggling your nose, clapping, waving) around the circle under the tent, from child to child.

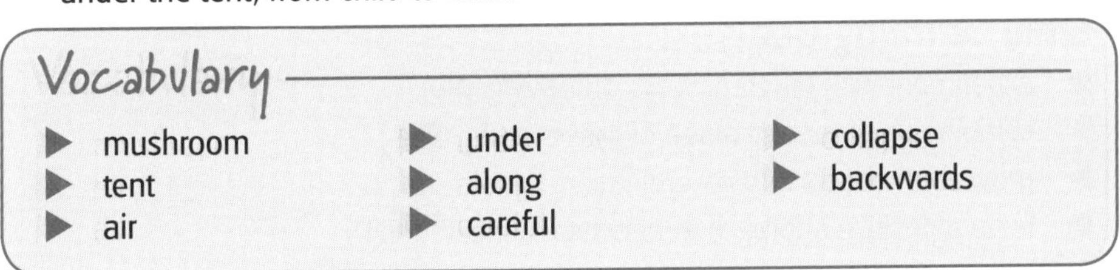

Vocabulary

- mushroom
- tent
- air
- under
- along
- careful
- collapse
- backwards

Pond life

These parachute games use favourite action songs and rhymes. Give your old favourites a new twist. There are many more well known rhymes suitable for parachute play.

What you need:

- just a parachute

Early Learning Goals:

- join in favourite songs; join in with repeated refrains. (CD)
- imitate and create movement in response to music; begin to move rhythmically. (CD)
- respond to simple instructions; Listen with enjoyment and respond to stories, songs and other music, rhymes and poems. (CLL)

What you do:

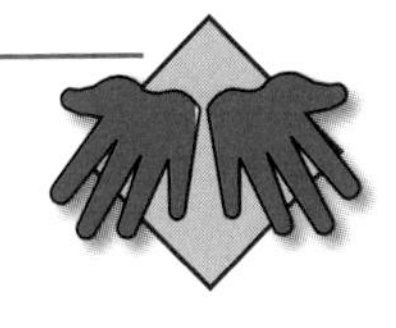

1. Spread the parachute on the floor and ask the children to sit around the edge.
2. Choose three children to be frogs.
3. Hold the parachute just a few cm above the ground and waft it gently to make the ripples on the pond.
4. Sing 'Three Little Speckled Frogs' (on the Carousel CD - see p68), with each frog jumping into and on the pond.

   Three little speckled frogs sat on a specked log,

   Eating some most delicious grubs.

   One jumped into the pool, where it was nice and cool,

   Then there were two green speckled frogs, glug, glug.
5. Each time you finish a verse, one child jumps out of your parachute pond and joins the group wafting the parachute. You can play this game with any number of frogs. Younger children may be best starting with three.

And another idea...

- Add some paper fishes to the pond. Sing '1, 2, 3, 4, 5, Once I Caught a Fish Alive!'
- Choose five children to be little ducks waddling around the pond and sing and do the actions of 'Five Little Ducks went Swimming one Day'.
- Make different sorts of waves on the pond. Can you make a still pond? Make the waves bigger and bigger, then smaller and smaller? Can you make huge slow waves, and fast smaller ripples?
- Sit the children close together in two groups on opposite sides of the parachute, with their legs stretched out under the parachute. Grip the parachute firmly, and rock backwards and forwards in a rowing action, singing 'Row, Row, Row your Boat, Gently Down the Stream'.

Vocabulary

- pond
- waves
- ripples
- fast
- slow
- choppy
- calm
- under

Set the sails – land ahoy!

Use your parachute to make a boat for a group of children. Makesome pirate props, climb aboard and sail away, singing your favourite sea songs and shanties.

What you need:

- a parachute
- a treasure chest or box
- pirate clothes, hats, ear-rings, 'telescopes' etc

Early Learning Goals:

- travel backwards and sideways as well as forwards. (PD)
- move with control and co-ordination. (PD)
- show awareness of space for themselves and others. (PD)
- collaborate in devising and sharing tasks, including those with rules. (PD)

What you do:

1. Make some props - telescopes from cardboard tubes, earrings from curtain rings on thin elastic, scarves for headdresses, etc.
2. Write the names of all the sea songs you know on bits of paper and put them in the treasure box.
3. Dress up in your pirate gear.
4. Lay the parachute flat on the floor. With another adult's help, roll and fold the sides of the parachute in to make an approximate rectangle shape.
5. Sit with the children on the parachute, in a line, one behind the other, all facing the same way. Lift the sides up to form the edge of the boat.
6. Ask one of the children to choose a slip of paper from the treasure chest. Sing the song, rocking the boat forwards and backwards together.
7. Try another song, rocking gently from side to side.
8. Try singing with one child standing up to look through their telescope as the boat moves from side to side in a storm!

And another idea...

- Cut an anchor shape from cardboard and attach it to the parachute with ribbon. Pull up the anchor on your boat, working together to heave the anchor up.
- Take a favourite sea story with you to read or tell as you gently rock from side to side.
- Make your own telescopes (decorated cardboard tubes, with cellophane lenses) and climb aboard the parachute ship. Help each child to in turn describe, but not name, what they can see through your telescope. Can the other children guess what they are looking at? You may need to help younger children by modelling this yourself.
- Use a rainmaker, shakers, drums or other musical instruments to describe the sea. Is it a calm pool, choppy sea, rolling waves, or a raging storm? Move the parachute together to match the sounds you can hear.

Vocabulary

- ocean
- sea
- waves
- treasure
- forwards
- backwards
- slowly/fast
- sideways

Traffic lights

Parachute play can help children to learn and understand games with rules. Here is one and some ideas for more. These games also help with listening skills.

What you need:

- 3 sound makers (eg a wooden block, shaker, bells, castanet)
- your parachute

Early Learning Goals:

- sustain attentive listening, responding to what they have heard. (PSED)
- respond to simple instructions; be confident to try new activities. (PSED)
- move with confidence and imagination and in safety; move freely with pleasure and confidence; stop; experiment with different ways of moving. (PD)

What you do:

1. Spread the parachute out on the floor and sit with the children around its edge.
2. Explain to the children that this is a listening game and when they hear the wooden blocks they need to lift the parachute as high as they can, while still staying seated. When they hear the shaker they need to shake the parachute vigorously at floor level, and when they hear the clicker or castanet, they need to lie back, still holding the parachute, and kick their legs up and down under the chute.
3. Start the game slowly, but gradually quicken the pace.
4. When they are confident with this game, try it with eyes closed!

And another idea...

- Play again with different instruments and big movements, such as standing up and sitting down with the parachute, letting go and swivelling right around when seated and then getting hold of the parachute again; and for the third action, lying flat on their tummies, arms stretched out in front of them. Get the children to suggest new actions.
- Put a red sticker on each child's right hand, and a blue sticker on their left. Hold the parachute at waist height. Play some music and travel in a circle. Call out 'red' and move to the right. When the music stops, call out red, or blue and then as soon as the music starts, continue around in the ring, in that direction.
- Hold the parachute at waist height and carefully roll the edges in, reducing the overall size of the parachute by about half. Hold onto the edge of the parachute. Ask the children to move together towards the door, for example, on tiptoe. Try moving forwards, backwards, or to different parts of the room. Use different ways of travelling while holding on to the parachute, such as bottom shuffling, giant strides, slithering and so on.

Vocabulary

- listen
- stop/go
- together
- fast/slow
- high
- low
- different
- next

Songs we know

Use your old favourites to make new parachute activities. You can often make a new song by changing just some of the words to make it fit the activity.

What you need:

- tickets for each child
- a horn or bell
- your parachute

Early Learning Goals:

- interact with others, negotiating plans and activities and taking turns in conversation (CLL)
- listen to favourite nursery rhymes, stories and songs; join in with repeated refrains, anticipating key events and important phrases. (CLL)
- respond to simple instructions; build up vocabulary; have a sense of belonging. (PSED)

What you do:

1. Spread the parachute on the floor and sit around the edge with the children.
2. Stand up and sing, 'The Wheels on the Bus go Round and Round'. To this, first move around in a circle. Sit for the next verse, and sing 'The Bell on the Bus Goes Ding, Ding Ding', passing the bell from child to child round the ring.
3. For the next verse, stand up and grip the parachute firmly and wave it from side to side – 'The Wipers on the Bus go Swish, Swish, Swish.'
4. Still holding the parachute, lie down so all the children's legs are under the parachute, as if they were fast asleep, and sing 'The Babies on the Bus go zzz.zzz,zzzz.'
5. Stand up and wave the parachute up and down, with the children jumping up and down and sing, 'The Children on the Bus Jump Up and Down'.
6. Finally, mushroom the parachute by holding it at waist height, wafting it high in the air and, as it billows, taking one step forward and quickly bringing the parachute down behind you and sitting on the edges. This may take some practice with the youngest children!
7. Pass the tickets around, so each child can take a ticket. Choose a driver to collect the tickets as you sing, 'The Driver on the Bus says Tickets Please!'

And another idea...

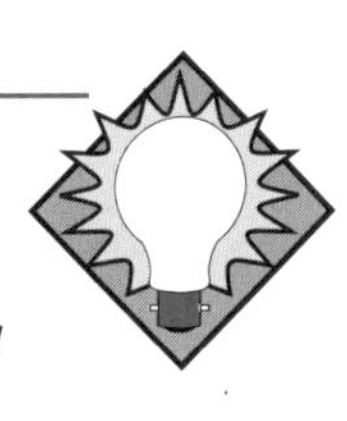

- Try 'Simon Says', with all the children holding the parachute. Include balancing positions such as 'Simon says stand on one leg', or 'Simon says wave your legs in the air'. They must follow all the actions without letting go of the parachute!
- 'Here We Go Round the Mulberry Bush' works well with the parachute. Sit on the floor, and during the chorus, instead of moving with the parachute, pass it around from hand-to-hand. Use actions that the children can do seated, such as rocking side to side, touching toes, bouncing on bottoms and so on.

Vocabulary

- turn
- listen
- action
- together
- let go
- hold on
- next
- share

Follow my leader

Another old favourite with a parachute twist. Follow my Leader gives children practice in imitating actions and taking turns.

What you need:

- a parachute
- small stickers (2 colours)
- soft balls (sponge or fabric)

Early Learning Goals:

- show respect for other children's personal space when playing among them. (PD)
- use increasing control over an object by touching, pushing, patting, throwing, catching and kicking it. (PD)
- interact with others, negotiating activities and taking turns in conversations. (CLL)
- respond to simple instructions. (PSED)

What you do:

1. Spread the parachute on the floor and sit around the edge with the children.
2. Give each child a sticker, alternating the two colours.
3. Stand up together, holding the parachute at about waist height. Throw the balls under the parachute.
4. Ask all the children with a sticker of one colour to let go of the parachute, find a ball and then come back to their place.
5. Now ask one child to be the leader, and weave in and out of the children holding the parachute, ducking under the parachute as necessary. The other children with the same colour sticker follow the leader.
6. Play again with the children with the other colour stickers.
7. This time the leader may kick the ball along, or perhaps hold it between their knees, or under an arm, as they weave their way in and out between the other children.
8. Try lots of different actions, perhaps hopping along, crawling, bottom shuffling and so on, forwards and backwards.

And another idea...

- Play again, with the leader changing their actions several times on the way around the circle.
- Lower the parachute close to the floor and ask the blues to cross under the parachute, perhaps on their backs, sliding along on their tummies, rolling over and over, and so on.
- Play follow my leader with balloons, with the leader travelling over and under the parachute with the balloon, perhaps tapping it from hand to hand, perhaps holding it between their elbows, perhaps with it behind their backs.
- Pass an action around the parachute. Hold the parachute at waist height and start by giving it a tiny shake. The child next to you copies this action and this continues until it gets back to you. Continue to play with different actions, such as lifting it high or low, stepping in or out, perhaps sitting down or jumping high.

Vocabulary

- leader
- copy
- watch
- look
- same
- similar
- like
- follow

Animals everywhere

Add some simple props to a parachute game to make a lively and creative activity.

What you need:

- a parachute
- squares of different fabric
- cardboard boxes
- ribbons and net

Early Learning Goals:

- enjoy joining in with dancing and ring games. (CD)
- begin to use representation as a means of communication. (CD)
- enter into dialogue about their creations. (CD)
- interact with others, taking turns in conversations. (CLL)
- use a widening range of words to express and elaborate ideas. (CLL)

What you do:

1. Place the fabrics and the boxes on the floor and spread the parachute over them.
2. Sit around the edge of the parachute with the children and talk about the different sorts of animals they know. What is their favourite animal? What do the animals look like? How do they move? What do they eat? Where do they sleep?
3. Stand up, holding the parachute at waist height. Waft the parachute high in the air and step sharply forwards, quickly bringing the parachute back down behind you, sitting down on the edge of it to make a mushroom tent.
4. Talk about the different fabrics and boxes you can see in front of you on the floor. Talk with them about how they can be used to help them pretend to be an animal at the zoo.
5. Sing together (to the tune of 'We Went to Visit the Farm One Day') 'We went to visit the zoo one day, we saw some elephants across the way, what do you think we saw them do? Swing, swing, swing', swinging your arm in front of you as a trunk. Invite two or three children to pretend to be an elephant, using any of the props they wish and creating their own actions. Sing the song again.
6. Take turns to be different animals, asking the children to predict what actions they might use for the animals.

And another idea...

- Make four outline cards of each of four animals. Give each child a card. Hold the parachute at waist height and wave it up and down. Call out one of the animal names, and help the children with that card to cross under the parachute to swap places with another child with the same card.
- Mushroom the parachute as described above and play 'One Elephant Went out to Play, Upon a Spider's Web One Day'.
- Create a dinosaur version of this game with different props and chant or sing, 'Long long ago, when the dinosaurs lived, out from the cave came the stegosaurus. What do you think he did?'

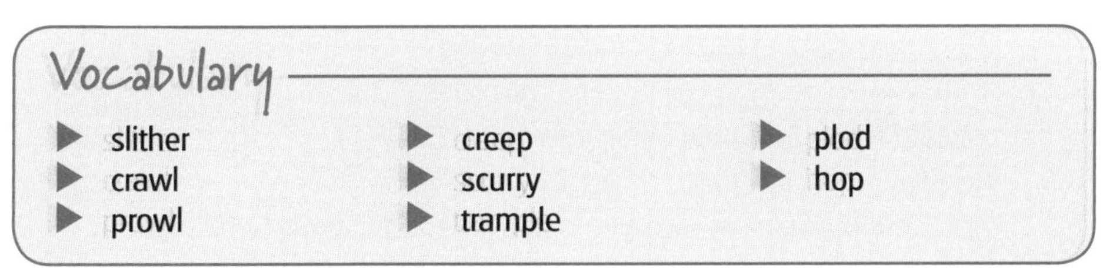

Postman's knock!

Not the old party version, but a way to practise first letter sounds, letters and names.

What you need:

- a parachute
- a shoulder bag
- a name card for each child
- Postman Pat music (if possible)

Early Learning Goals:

- hear and say initial sounds in words; know which letter represents some sounds. (CLL)
- begin to recognise some familiar words. (CLL)
- form good relationships with adults and peers. (PSED)
- relate and make attachments to members of their group. (PSED)

What you do:

1. Put the children's name cards in a pile.
2. Turn these over one by one, and as each child recognises their own name, let them put it in the bag. Talk about the first letters and first letter sounds on each name card.
3. Spread the parachute on the floor and stand around the edge with the children. Lift the parachute to waist height.
4. Give the bag to one of the children to be 'Postie'.
5. Play the Postman Pat music, or sing the song, as you move around in a circle with the parachute.
6. Stop the music. Ask 'Postie' to take a name card, and hold it up for all the children to see. That child then has to race the Postie around the circle back to their original place.
7. Pass the bag to the next child and play again. Continue until the bag is empty and all the children have had a turn. Keep changing the direction the circle is moving in.

And another idea...

- Can the children side-step or skip to the music and sit down as soon as it stops?
- Pull two name cards from the bag, and ask these children to run under the parachute to swap places.
- Place all the name cards face up on the floor under the parachute. Sit down and hold the parachute about 30cm off the floor. Invite children in groups of three to dive under the parachute and find their name.
- Waft the parachute up and down, and then call out "If your name begins with 'S', dive under. Let the parachute fall gently onto the heads of the children who have dived under the parachute. Bring it up slowly and check that you have caught the right children in the middle!
- Give all the children paper, pen and an old envelope. Ask them to write a note or draw a picture, then pull a name card from the bag. Copy this name onto their envelope. Take turns to deliver the notes and drawings in their envelopes by running round or under the parachute.

Vocabulary

- letter
- sound
- word
- name
- listen
- find
- pass
- turn

All dressed up

Use your parachute to help the children to practice dressing up skills and helping each other. Add some unusual things such as flippers, arm bands, wellies, fluffy slippers, long socks, raincoats, hats, wigs etc.

What you need:

- a parachute
- dressing up clothes with easy fastenings
- a sand or other timer

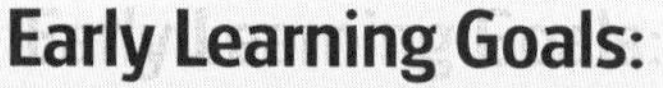

Early Learning Goals:

- dress and undress independently; show confidence in linking up with others. (PSED)
- show willingness to tackle problems; show care and concern for others. (PSED)
- speak clearly and audibly with confidence and control and show awareness of the listener; use terms such as please and thank you. (CLL)

What you do:

1. Spread out the parachute on the floor.
2. Ask everyone to choose a dressing up item, bring it over to the parachute and sit around the edge.
3. Ask the child next to you to stand up. Set the timer going and ask that child to put on their dressing up clothes, with the help of the child next to them.
4. As soon as they are finished, the next child puts on their dressing up clothes, with the help of the next child, and so on.
5. Continue round the parachute. Can you make it right around the circle before the timer is finished?
6. Next, lift the parachute together and waft it up and down.
7. When it is high in the air, call out an item of clothing (e.g.'hat'). All the children with hats have to let go and cross over under the parachute, before the chute falls to the floor.

And another idea...

- Spread out the parachute on the floor and place a different item of dressing up clothing on each coloured segment. Call out the names of two children and ask them to dress up in all the items on, say, red segments. Ask other pairs of children to work together to dress up in the clothes on the blue sections, and so on.
- Choose one child to be dressed. Ask him or her to stand in the middle of the parachute. Give all the children around the edge a different item of clothing. Ask the child in the centre to call out the name of the child holding something for, perhaps, a rainy day. The child in the centre then calls out the name of the child holding dressing up clothes for a rainy day. This child then crawls into the middle and helps the first child put on the rainy day clothes. Continue to add more and more clothes to the child in the middle, asking them to find clothes of different colours, textures, for different weather or activities, and so on.
- Put hats and shoes under the parachute. Ask all the children wearing blue today to find a hat, then all the children wearing yellow to find a shoe. Continue with other colours.

Vocabulary

- fastener words
- top
- bottom
- help
- sleeve
- together
- body parts
- next

First letter sounds

Explore everyday objects and listen for first letter sounds with this parachute game. You need some small objects with clear single sounds at the beginning of their names.

What you need:

- a parachute
- a shoe box with a lid
- small objects such as an apple, ball, car, toy dog, egg, fish

Early Learning Goals:

- ask simple questions, extend vocabulary, especially by grouping and naming. (CLL)
- build up a vocabulary that reflects the breadth of their experiences. (CLL)
- use vocabulary focused on objects and people who are important to them. (CLL)
- link sounds to letters; hear and say initial letter sound in words and know which letters represent some of the sounds. (CLL)

What you do:

1. Show the children the objects you will use and help them to say the first letter sound of each one.
2. Mushroom the parachute by wafting it high in the air, stepping forward, quickly bringing it down behind you and sitting on the edge. The air trapped inside the parachute creates a mushroom or tent. Remind the children to stay seated, or the air will escape and the parachute will collapse!
3. Place three or four of your objects in the box, put the lid on, and slide the box across the parachute tent to a child.
4. Ask the child to look inside the box and tell everyone the first letter sound of one of the objects it contains. Can the children guess what it might be? Give clues and prompts, such as, 'Is it something that you can eat?' Encourage the child to describe the object by its use, colour, shape, etc.
5. When one of the children guesses correctly, slide the box over to that child and continue to play the game. Add more objects to the box as necessary.

And another idea...

- Give all the children a small picture of an object (perhaps from a lotto or pairs game). Ask them to call out the name of the object and the first letter sound. Then pick up the parachute and pull it taut. Hold it with just one hand each and walk in one direction around the circle. Every so often, stop and call out a first letter sound. Children with pictures of objects with that first letter sound quickly cross over under the parachute to the opposite side, and continue to play the game.
- Play the same game, but this time ask the children to cross over if their object is used in, say, the garden, kitchen, etc.
- Give each child a post-it note with a letter on. Use pairs of letters so that you can call out different letters and ask the children to swap places.

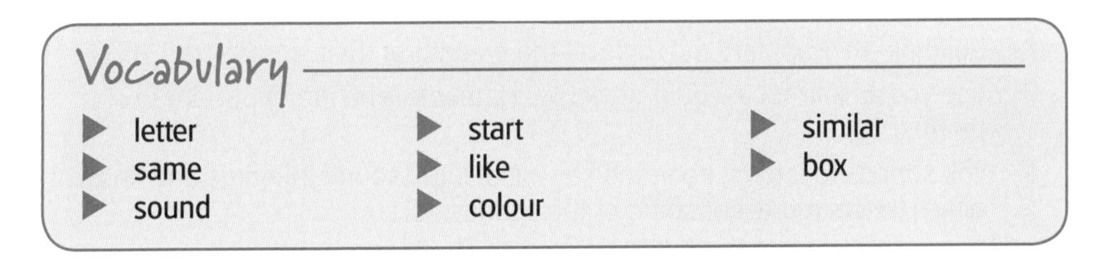

Up and down, side to side

Get physical with this lively game – marching, kicking, hopping and stamping. It also helps with listening!

What you need:

- a parachute
- simple instruments (shaker, tambourine, bells etc)
- drum music on CD or tape

Early Learning Goals:

- move with confidence, imagination and in safety; go backwards and sideways as well as forwards; stop; move in a range of ways; negotiate space. (PD)
- work as part of a group, or class; show care and concern for others. (PSED)
- consider the consequences of their words and actions for others. (PSED)

What you do:

1. Spread out the parachute and sit around it with the children. Pick the parachute up and hold it taut between you.
2. Stretch your legs under the parachute, keeping it taut.
3. Start the drum music, and kick to the rhythm under the parachute.
4. Next, stand up and pull the parachute taut again. Let go of the parachute with one hand and stand side on to it, all facing in the same direction.
5. March to the drum music, but ask the children to listen out for the bell, shaker or other instrument. When they hear this, they should swap hands, turn around and change direction.
6. Try this several times with one instrument before adding another sound to the game. When the children hear the next sound, they should quickly sit down and stand up again and (when the child next to them is ready), continue marching.
7. Quicken the pace for older or more mature children.
8. Emphasise the importance of looking out for other children (e.g. the child on each side) and working as part of a team.

And another idea...

- Practice moving forwards and backwards, in and out of the circle with the parachute. Try crawling forwards and backwards, holding the parachute – giant strides, jumping, or even bunny hops!
- Hold the parachute and chant with actions – 'Up and down, up and down, side to side, side to side, here we go again. Up and down, up and down, side to side, this is where we stop!'
- Play cross over games with the children choosing different actions, such as rolling, commando crawling, slithering, swimming, walking on heels, crawling backwards, and so on.
- Play musical bumps. When the music stops all the children dive down under the parachute, leaving the adults holding the parachute above their heads. Ask the children to sit in different positions – legs outstretched, kneeling, legs crossed.

Vocabulary

- drum
- slow
- beat
- listen
- rhythm
- follow
- fast
- next

In the band

Making music and changing sounds are the focus of this game where you can use all sorts of sound makers, not just instruments.

What you need:

- a parachute
- sound makers (blocks, keys, spoons, pans, balloons. etc.)
- simple musical instruments

Early Learning Goals:

- show an interest in the way musical instruments sound; begin to build a repertoire of songs; explore and learn how sounds can be changed. (CD)
- continue to be interested, excited and motivated to learn; be confident to try new activities. (PSED)

What you do:

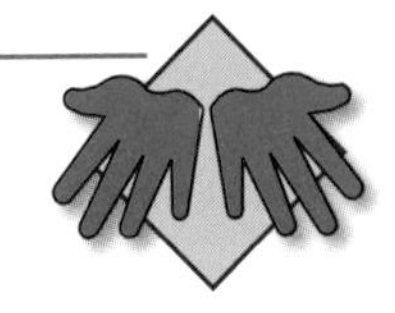

1. Spread out the parachute on the floor and ask each of the children to sit on a different coloured section.
2. Place all the instruments and sound makers in the middle.
3. Sing 'I am the music man, I come from far away, and I can play. What can you play? I can play the ....' Ask a child to choose an instrument.
4. Talk about the different sounds this instrument makes, such as the bang of the drum. Ask all the children on the blue sections to find something from the middle to make a drum – like sound (tapping on a balloon, banging blocks together).
5. Sing the verse again, and when it gets to the last line, ask each child to play in turn ('I can play the drum', 'I can play the balloon', 'I can play the blocks', etc.)
6. Continue to play the game until all the children have had a turn with the instruments and sound makers.
7. Next, adults hold the parachute high. Ask the drummer to lead the children around and under the parachute, follow my leader style, as you all sing 'We are the music men, we come from far away, and we can play....'

And another idea...

- Stand in a circle, eyes closed, holding the parachute taut. Have one child with a chime bar and beater walk slowly around the outside of the circle. Let them strike the chime bar behind a child of their choosing. This is a signal for them to put down the chime bar and race around the outside of the parachute with the other child, trying to get back to that child's place before them.
- Sit down and hold the parachute taut just above ground level. Add tiny bells and soft squeaky toys to the top of the parachute. How can you change the sounds they make?
- Hold the parachute taut, just high enough for children to wriggle under. Hide some sound makers and instruments under the parachute. Invite a child to wriggle under, fetch one and slither to the other side without making a sound.

Vocabulary

- loud/soft
- clang
- high/low
- hiss
- beat
- shake
- ring
- rattle

Count down!

Use your parachute to help with counting and number recognition in these simple games.

What you need:

- a parachute
- a large floor dice – numbers or dots
- plastic bricks or counters
- number cards 1–6

Early Learning Goals:

- count up to six objects from a larger group; recognise numerals; say and use number names in order in familiar contexts. (PSRN)
- use language such as 'more' or 'less' to compare two numbers. (PSRN)
- work as part of a group or class taking turns and sharing fairly. (PSED)

What you do:

1. Spread out the parachute on the floor.
2. Stand around the edge with the children and lift the parachute to child waist height. Spread plastic bricks or counters around under the parachute. Put the number cards on the floor outside the parachute circle.
3. Take turns to throw the dice and count the number of spots together. The dice thrower then dives under the parachute to collect that number of bricks or counters. As they dive under the parachute, waft it up and down in huge movements, or dance around in a circle.
4. Next, ask that child to count the number of bricks they have collected and place it on the card with the correct numeral.
5. Continue to take turns to throw the dice until all the cards have the right number of bricks. If a number is thrown that has already been completed, pass the dice to the next child.
6. Play again till everyone has had a turn.

And another idea...

- Bounce a large soft foam dice on top of the parachute. When it bounces off, count the number of spots, and that number of children need to let go of the parachute and sit in the middle underneath it. The remaining children will need to spread out to hold the parachute. Continue to play until the parachute finally collapses on the children in the middle!
- Throw a dice and count the spots. Place that number of small soft toys on the parachute and bounce them gently up and down. Keep throwing the dice and adding more soft toys – how many can you bounce without any falling off?
- Give each child a numbered sticker from one to six (or one to ten). Sit around the edge of the parachute and shake it gently to make the ripples on a pond or sea. Sing 1, 2, 3, 4, 5, Once I Caught a Fish Alive. When each child's number is sung, they need to jump into the pond and continue singing the rhyme from the middle of the pond.

Vocabulary

- more
- same
- less
- count
- guess
- turn
- estimate
- number

Minibeasts

This game can link with a popular topic, providing active, whole body play to reinforce learning.

What you need:

- a parachute
- a spider puppet, soft toy or home made spider
- a piece of card in the shape of the sun

Early Learning Goals:

- comment and ask questions about the natural world; show an interest in the world in which they live; investigate objects and materials by using all senses. (KUW)
- listen with enjoyment, and respond to stories, songs and other music, rhymes and poems; use a widening range of words to express and elaborate ideas. (CLL)

What you do:

1. Sit on the edge of the parachute and gently pass the spider from one child to the next. When everyone has had a chance to hold the spider, ask one of the children to crawl onto the parachute with it. Talk about how a spider might move.
2. Now give small groups of three or four children a chance to move around on top of the parachute, trying out spider moves.
3. Invite a second child to hold the sun shape and sing 'Incey, Wincey Spider'. Do the actions together.
4. Experiment making rain sounds with the parachute - rubbing the material together, or tapping or kicking it as it is held taut. The 'sunshine' can pop up through the central hole in the parachute.
5. Finish with a chasing parachute game. Hold the parachute at waist level with one child with the spider underneath. Tell the others they are a fly, a ladybird, or a bluebottle.
6. Call out one of the insects. These children need to cross under the parachute without being caught by the spider. If they are caught, let them rejoin the game for another turn.
7. Take turns to be the spider, continuing the game until everyone has had a chance to try to escape the spider's clutches several times.

And another idea...

- Read 'The Very Hungry Caterpillar' by Eric Carle or 'The Crunching Munching Caterpillar' by Sheridan Cain and Jack Tickle. Take turns under the parachute to be wriggling caterpillars, squirming and writhing along. Give the children chiffon scarves or similar fabric so they can become butterflies emerging from their cocoons.
- Mushroom the parachute and sit inside. Say the rhyme by Ian Serrallier, 'Who's that ticking my back? says the wall. It's me, says the caterpillar, I'm learning to crawl.' Make tiny finger caterpillars and crawl up the wall of the parachute, then to the right and then to the left. Make them crawl along your legs right down to your toes.

Vocabulary

- spider
- creeping
- moving
- crawling
- legs
- wriggling
- web
- catch

Up and down parachute hill

A game for investigating rolling, using a parachute for a different purpose.

What you need:

- a parachute
- strong tape, scissors, chalk
- small cars, balls, card tubes, bean bags

Early Learning Goals:

- investigate objects and materials by using all of their senses as appropriate; look closely at similarities, differences and change; ask questions about why things happen and how things work. (KUW)
- use everyday words to describe position; use developing mathematical ideas and methods to solve practical problems. (PSRN)

What you do:

1. Fix one edge of the parachute securely to a steady table, storage unit or frame, at about table height. Secure the rest of the parachute with tape to the floor, pulling it taut to make a hill.
2. Make a target using chalk or tape to circle some way from the bottom of the parachute.
3. Ask each child to choose a car or other object to roll down the hill. Ask them to choose something that they think may roll into the target area. Talk about the reasons for their choices. Try to ask open questions and encourage the children to think ahead, predict and develop their ideas.
4. Take turns to release the objects down your parachute hill. Encourage each child to mark where their object has landed, writing or copying from their name cards on to a label fixed to the floor or with chalk.
5. Try different objects and help the children to work out why some objects roll closer to the target than others.
6. Ask the children to choose a car. Add their name on a sticky label and race the cars down the hill.

And another idea...

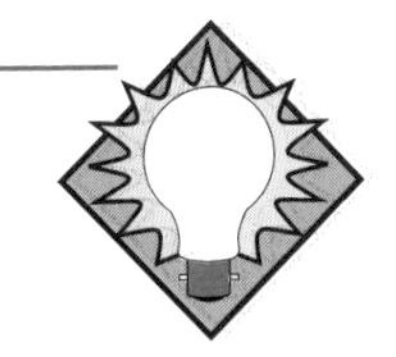

- Try varying the steepness of the hill. Ask the children for ideas on how to vary the gradient – could you put a box under the parachute hill to make a hump on the track?
- Ask the children to work in pairs rolling balls up and down the hill to each other.
- Add a wooden train set and encourage the children to try and build a track up the hill.
- Use tape or ribbon to mark lanes on the hill. Roll the cars down the hill, counting how many get down staying in lane and how many cross over lanes. Use a clip board to record the results.

Vocabulary

- steep
- smooth
- fast/slow
- bumpy
- light/heavy
- near/far
- round
- up/down

Target time

Use your parachute to give children eye/hand co-ordination practice with these target games and activities.

What you need:

- a parachute
- rolled up pairs of socks
- small soft balls, quoits, rings
- balloons or beach balls

Early Learning Goals:

- retrieve, collect and catch objects; use increasing control over an object, by touching, pushing, patting, throwing, catching and kicking it; persevere in repeating some actions/attempts when developing a new skill; show respect for other children's personal space when playing among them; move body position as necessary. (PD)

What you do:

1. Spread out the parachute on the floor and ask a child to sit near the centre, one on each coloured segment.
2. Sit a partner for each child at the outside edge of each coloured segment.
3. Practice rolling the beach balls between the partners along each coloured segment. Call out a colour and ask the children on that segment to roll the ball to their partner. Call out different colours for different children, in quick succession.
4. Next, try throwing the ball to each other. Play the game, calling out different colours and 'roll' or 'throw' – so the children need to listen for both parts of the instruction.
5. Try adding the rings, rolled up socks and the beach balls. Practice rolling, throwing and catching.

And another idea...

- Play the same game, kicking the beach balls to each other, or patting the balloons.
- Mushroom the parachute by wafting it high into the air, then step forward, pull the parachute down behind you and sit down on the edge of the parachute. The trapped air will create a mushroom or tent. The children need to stay seated or the air will escape and the mushroom will collapse! Place a ring or quoit on the first child's arm and ask them to pass it to the child next to them by sliding the ring down their arm and onto their neighbour's. Continue to pass the ring around the circle. Try passing rings from foot to foot, too!
- Practice rolling balls across the circle inside the mushroomed parachute.
- Spread out the parachute on the floor and sort coloured beanbags on to matching coloured segments. Next take turns to try and throw the beanbags into the hole at the centre of the parachute.

Vocabulary

- throw
- near/far
- catch
- fast/slow
- hands
- roll
- under/over
- bounce

Full of beans

Play a new version of the Hokey Cokey in this singing game with plenty of action!

What you need:

- a parachute
- a bell or chime bar

Early Learning Goals:

- adjust speed and change direction to avoid obstacles; go backwards and side ways as well as forwards; experiment with different ways of moving; show awareness of space, of themselves and of others. (PD)
- have a developing awareness of their own needs, views and feelings and be sensitive to the needs, views and feelings of others. (PSED)

What you do:

1. Spread out the parachute on the ground and sit around it with the children.
2. Tell the children that you are going to do the hokey-cokey with the parachute, and ask them to help you work out some rules that will make it safe for everyone – such as stopping if the person next to you falls over, taking care not to bump into others and so on.
3. Lift the parachute to waist height and sing the song.
4. Encourage the children to use big exaggerated movements, and praise them for adjusting their own actions to fit their neighbour's.
5. Practice turning around, holding the chute with first one hand then the other as you turn.
6. Sound the bell or chime bar at frequent intervals to indicate that the children should change the direction of the circle. Encourage them to keep hold of the parachute at all times.

And another idea...

- Drape the parachute over some boxes to create a tunnel. Try scrambling under the tunnel – forwards, backwards, sideways, on tummies, bottoms, hands and knees, or hands and feet.
- Play a cross over game, where children whose name begins with a particular first letter sound swap places under the parachute, crossing over in a specified way, such as slithering backwards, crawling sideways, jumping, hopping, skipping, etc.
- With some adult helpers, hold the parachute just a little way above the height the children can reach. Ask the children to jump up at the edges and throw some balloons or soft toys onto the top of the chute. Next ask them to jump up under the chute to try and knock the balloons or soft toys to the side, and eventually off the parachute.

Vocabulary

- in/out
- backwards
- up/down
- neighbour
- side to side
- space
- forwards
- carefully

Reach for the sky!

Parachute games are good for big body movements. Try this one for stretching and jumping.

What you need:

- a parachute
- plenty of energy!

Early Learning Goals:

- show awareness of space, or themselves and of others; move with control and co-ordination; experiment with different ways of moving; adjust speed or change direction to avoid obstacles. (PD)
- express and communicate their ideas, by using a widening range of imaginative and role-play and movement. (CD)

What you do:

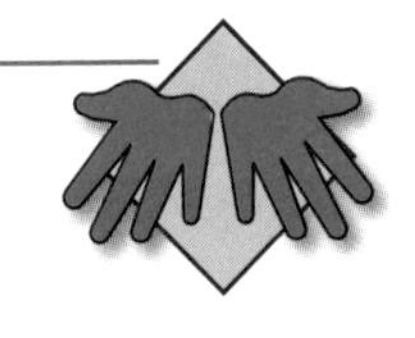

1. Sit around the edge of the parachute and think with the children of different animals that jump – kangaroos, rabbits, jumping spiders, frogs, etc.
2. Try out different ways that the animals might jump – on all fours, with two feet together, feet apart, legs straight, legs bent and so on.
3. With other adults, hold the parachute high in the air and call out 'jumping spider', 'kangaroo', 'rabbit', 'frog' , etc.
4. The children jump around under the chute in the style of that animal. See if they can jump so their heads touch the underneath of the chute.
5. Next think of tall animals, such as elephants, horses and giraffes. Talk about and try out the way they can move. Stretch arms and legs to make big shapes and long tails. Strut about under the parachute, reaching high and pretending to be one of the animals.

And another idea...

- Stand, holding the chute up high. Invite a child to cross under the parachute, singing 'My name is ..., and I can jump high.' They jump across to another child, who then jumps back under the parachute to another child, perhaps doing bunny jumps, or tiny little jumps.
- Invite half the children to curl up really small on the floor. Hold the parachute with the other children, so it is resting gently on the backs of the curled up children. Chant 'Small, small small, getting taller, taller, taller, tall, tall tall', gradually lifting the parachute as the children uncurl and stretch up as tall as they can. Lower the parachute, gently reversing, 'Tall, tall tall, getting small, small, small'.
- Spread the parachute on the floor and invite a child to lie on a segment, feet pointing towards the centre. Ask them to spread their arms wide. Invite another child to lie down next to them so their stretched arms touch their fingertips. How many children do you need to complete the parachute circle?

Vocabulary

- high/low
- curled
- straight
- tall
- bent
- small
- stretched
- under

Using your parachute every day

Having bought or made a parachute for your reception, nursery or preschool group, you will want to make the most of it. The parachute can be used for all sorts of games and activities to support learning in all six areas of learning.

Incorporate your parachute in themes and topics

Parachute games can be planned to fit with topics and theme work. They can be used to help you organise your space, define new and interesting play areas and as a part of displays.

Here are some ideas:

Fix your parachute securely to the ceiling to create a tent or big top. This could make a great imaginative play area. Try using it as:

- big top for circus performers
- a tent for camping holidays
- an alternative home corner
- the sails of a ship
- a café
- the inside of a space shuttle
- a jungle

Use your parachute to make a special place

Define new areas for:

- using real and improvised musical instruments
- rest and relaxation with story tapes, books and soft toys
- a special story time

Use your parachute to spotlight or revive an area

Brighten up existing areas with a parachute backdrop – think how you could use the parachute in:

- the mark-making corner
- the collage and paint area
- with bricks and construction

Make an entrance

Make an entrance special with the parachute draped over. Leave plenty of headroom for adults to walk safely under the parachute's folds.

Take it outside

Plan to use the parachute outside, not just for games – but try it as:

- a billowing sail
- a tunnel
- a canopy at different heights
- a hammock

Stay safe!

Make sure the parachute is fixed securely at all times. Think ahead to avoid potential accidents. Check any concerns with a senior member of staff who has responsibility for health and safety in your setting.

Make some mini-parachutes

Try making some mini parachutes with coloured fabric. These are ideal for activities in small spaces with just two or three children, or perhaps, even one to one.

Make some mini-parachutes

Why not make a black and white patterned parachute? Help visually impaired children by creating a parachute from some fluorescent or bright yellow fabric, and perhaps add a textured braid around the edge.

Long and thin

Try some of the parachute games with long narrow lengths of fabric, say 1 metre wide, and five metres long.

Resources and contacts

For a list of toy libraries near you, contact the local Children's Information Service, listed in Yellow Pages, or log on to web site www.childcarelink.gov.uk, or call 08000 96 02 96

Alternatively, contact the National Association of Toy Libraries, 68 Churchway, London NW1 1TL Tel: 020 7387 9592, web site www.natll.org.uk

Thinking of buying a parachute? Here's a quick checklist

1. Decide where you are going to use the parachute and measure the smallest of these spaces. You will need plenty of space around the parachute free of obstacles and potential hazards
2. Look for a parachute that is made of a strong but light fabric.
3. Check that the seams are fixed securely. They need to be strong enough to take plenty of active play.
4. Can you specify the colours when you order?
5. If you have a child with a visual impairment, why not think of bright or fluorescent colours for the parachute? Try to choose panels of sharply contrasting colours.
6. Think about how you want to use the parachute. This may influence your choice of design and size.

Where to buy a parachute

You will find parachutes in the catalogues of most educational suppliers. Try:

ASCO Educational Supplies
19 Lockwood Way, Leeds, LS11 5THE
Tel: 0113 270 7070

Galt Educational and Preschool Supplies
Johnson Brook Rd, Hyde, Cheshire. SK14 4QT
Tel: 08451 203005

GLS Educational Supplies, 1 Mollinson AveEnfield, Middlesex
EN3 7QS Tel: 020 8805 8333
website: www.glsed.co.uk

Hope Educational Supplies
Hyde Buildings, Ashton Rd, Hyde, Cheshire SK14 4SH
website: www.hope-education.co.uk

NES Arnold
Findel House, Excelsior Way, Ashby de la Zouch,
Leicestershire LE65 1NG
Tel: 0845 204525
website: www.nesarnold.co.uk

For bespoke parachutes, try

Seamstress Ltd
23 Banbury Rd, Byfield, Northants NN11 6XJ
Tel: 0137 263933
website: www.playchutes.com

More titles in the Little Books series include ...

LB Dance

ISBN 978-1-9041-8774-5

LB Bags, Boxes and Trays

ISBN 978-1-9050-1909-0

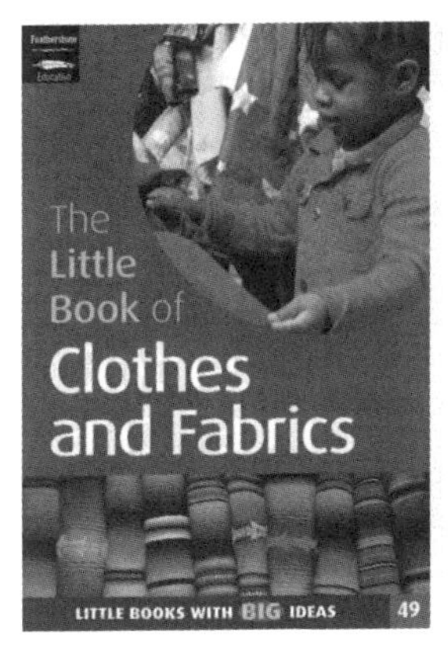

LB Clothes and Fabrics

ISBN 978-1-9050-1969-4

LB Sound Ideas

ISBN 978-1-9050-1955-7

All available from

www.acblack.com/featherstone

If you have found this book useful you might also like ...

LB Making Poetry

ISBN 978-1-4081-1250-2

LB Christmas

ISBN 978-1-9022-3364-2

LB Discovery Bottles

ISBN 978-1-9060-2971-5

LB Music

ISBN 978-1-9041-8754-7

All available from

www.acblack.com/featherstone

The Little Books Club

There is always something in Little Books to help and inspire you. Packed full of lovely ideas, Little Books meet the need for exciting and practical activities that are fun to do, address the Early Learning Goals and can be followed in most settings. Everyone is a winner!

We publish 5 new Little Books a year. Little Books Club members receive each of these 5 books as soon as they are published for a reduced price. The subscription cost is £37.50 – a one off payment that buys the 5 new books for £7.50 instead of £8.99 each.

In addition to this, Little Books Club Members receive:

- Free postage and packing on anything ordered from the Featherstone catalogue
- A 15% discount voucher upon joining which can be used to buy any number of books from the Featherstone catalogue
- Members price of £7.50 on any additional Little Book purchased
- A regular, free newsletter dealing with club news, special offers and aspects of Early Years curriculum and practice
- All new Little Books on approval - return in good condition within 30 days and we'll refund the cost to your club account

Call 020 7440 2446 or email: littlebooks@acblack.com for an enrolment pack. Or download an application form from our website:

www.acblack.com/featherstone

The **Little Books** series consists of:

All Through the Year
Bags, Boxes & Trays
Bricks and Boxes
Celebrations
Christmas
Circle Time
Clay and Malleable Materials
Clothes and Fabrics
Colour, Shape and Number
Cooking from Stories
Cooking Together
Counting
Dance
Dance, with music CD
Discovery Bottles
Dough
50
Fine Motor Skills
Fun on a Shoestring
Games with Sounds
Growing Things
ICT
Investigations
Junk Music
Language Fun
Light and Shadow
Listening
Living Things
Look and Listen
Making Books and Cards
Making Poetry
Mark Making
Maths Activities
Maths from Stories
Maths Songs and Games
Messy Play
Music
Nursery Rhymes
Outdoor Play
Outside in All Weathers
Parachute Play
Persona Dolls
Phonics
Playground Games
Prop Boxes for Role Play
Props for Writing
Puppet Making
Puppets in Stories
Resistant Materials
Role Play
Sand and Water
Science through Art
Scissor Skills
Sewing and Weaving
Small World Play
Sound Ideas
Storyboards
Storytelling
Seasons
Time and Money
Time and Place
Treasure Baskets
Treasureboxes
Tuff Spot Activities
Washing Lines
Writing

All available from

www.acblack.com/featherstone